Thirty and Single

*Your Guide to Living a Fulfilled Life while **Waiting***

Crystal Hall

ISBN-13: 978-0692281758

ISBN 10: 0692281754

Dedication

This book is dedicated to All Women struggling with their position in life. I want you to know you are not alone and that all you have to do is stay faithful. I'm praying for each and every one of you. Just trust the process. Love you sis!

Acknowledgments

Dear Heavenly Father, I want to just say Thank you. Thank you for who you are and what you've done to give me and everyone the newness of life. I am so thankful for your unconditional love. Even when I thought I was all alone you reminded me that you are always there for me. Thank you for my portion and my journey, Lord, I trust you.

I would just like to take the time out to acknowledge some very special people who encouraged, supported and loved me through everything.

To my Parents, Brenda Sanders and Harold Hall, I Thank you for raising into the woman I am today. Without your constant love and support I don't think I could've done half of the things I have done in my 32 years on earth. Mommy, you are a true inspiration. I love you both.

To my Pastors and the whole Living Faith Church, The support and love you all show is priceless. The teaching and motivation helped mold me to be who I have become. This partnership I have with Living Faith Church is the best partnership I have ever done. I am so blessed to have a loving church family!

To my Brothers, Oh Boy!! I love you guys. The Saturday morning cartoons on Monica, the cutting of my pig tails, the countless pranks and torture from being your only sister are priceless moments that will never be forgotten. Thank you for your support and love. I pray for you guys all the time rather near or far. Love your little BIG sister!

To my "Granny Boo", That mouth of yours is going to get you in some trouble lol. But I Thank God daily that he has allowed me to have you all this time. Through countless health scares God has always wrapped his loving arms around you and kept you for me. God is a GREAT God!!! When I look at you I look at how God has truly kept you in tip top condition. Girl you're blessed and have so many testimonies not only for you to tell but I attest to them and shout them from the mountain top. We are so blessed to have our granny around. I pray for you daily and I love you very much so. Ms. Sista *wink*

To my little heart -MY NEPHEW, Whew this is where it gets real. I don't know where to start. You're not old enough to read this and understand it, but I didn't know love could be such a blessed feeling. You are my heart and all of what I do is for you. I understand when parents talk about their children and tears begin to fall from their eyes. I may not be a biological mom, but I know what it feels like when a mom loves her son. When you get old enough and can look back and read this know that you are so loved. This may sound cliché but you truly brighten my day and my life. I love you Jay.

Table of Contents

5

6

7

8

9

10

Introduction

I am sitting on my couch just getting back from a weekend getaway. I decided to travel four hours outside of Detroit, Michigan, to the Upper Peninsula to get some "me" time and clarity. My main focus was to relax and hear from God without any distractions. It had been on my heart for many years to write this book but I could not focus on it. I knew what I wanted to write but just was not sure how to formulate all my rambled thoughts into book form. I am no journalist nor am I the perfect writer, but I am in a particular season of life and I have the desire to write about it. I can relate to it. I am thirty-one years old, single, have no biological children and I feel like my clock is a ticking time bomb. I am surrounded by many friends who are either married, engaged, expecting or in a courtship on its way to marriage.

I am not an expert on the single life and I do not have it all figured out on learning how to accept it for the time being. But, I am single and it seems to not be getting any easier. It has become so called "common wisdom" that by the time you are in your late twenties you should have at least one child and a husband. I was told I had to follow this timeline no matter what and it had to be completed in a timely manner. The focus was never on getting me prepared for this lifestyle of so called bliss. The focus was always on finding a man and settling down despite the circumstances. Just have somebody; ANYBODY. I was not enjoying my life I was merely trying to force my wants and beliefs on men, and in the process I was defiling myself little by little. Each time I pushed closer to this expectation, I pushed myself away from the enjoyment of life and the possible enjoyment of true love. I was forcing it and losing myself in the process.

Thirty and Single: Your Guide to Living a Fulfilled Life while **Waiting,** is a special book. This book is dedicated to the single woman in her thirties who may be experiencing loneliness, depression, anger, pressure and the feelings of being unfulfilled. I am willing to tell my story, lend an ear and give my opinion on how to live a fulfilled single life while we are waiting. Sometimes we just need someone who is standing directly in our shoes. It is not a knock on anyone else, it is just easier to receive truth from someone one who understands. So, I encourage you to find a quiet spot, get a warm cup of tea, a pen or pencil and begin your journey with me. We will laugh together, maybe even cry. We will reflect and may even become frustrated, but we will do it all together. It is time to heal, ladies, and live our lives. Single life should not feel like a death sentence. It is actually a time for you to get to know YOU, your wants from love, and your needs from love. To find a way to accomplish the purpose that is within. If we continue to look down on being single we will not accomplish anything and life will just pass us by. Let's not be those women who sit idle and stop living. There is a life to be created. We are given life, now we must make God proud by creating the best possible life we can. You do not have to wait for it. You have already been given access to it. Now, let's do it justice.

I pray you enjoy this book and learn something from it, be it learning how to move forward from your past or simply how to enjoy life. Whatever lessons learned will help you and me into the next level of our lives.

1

Wait?

Waiting too many people mean to sit idle at a pause and not do anything. And yes many dictionary definitions says that to be true. But I have found that waiting does not have to mean to sit idle. I have taken the word waiting and created something that means the total opposite. Waiting in my mind means giving your cares of singleness over to the Lord and work on living your life. Not allowing a single moment to pass you by. We get so overwhelmed with that word SINGLE that it haunts us. We become depressed, angry, frustrated, worried and anxious just because we do not have somebody. We continually chase after love even when we are empty on the inside and know that we are not ready for real *agape* love. Besides that, we do not even know how to love. We have been covering up are true selves for so long we cannot figure out who we are and what we truly want. When we look back we notice we have settled many times for what is given. We do not fully enjoy life because we are constantly *waiting* on the generic way for love. Many of us, myself included, have not given ourselves enough time to learn who we are. As a matter of fact we are not taught to enjoy who we are.

From birth we are conditioned to become mothers and wives. We go through life hoping and praying that we find "Mr. Right" and that we find him by a certain age. And, if we do not our lives immediately become stagnant and complacent because our whole lives revolve around changing our last name. We allow our happiness to be dependent upon rather we have a man or not. That is not how life is envisioned for us, being God's daughters. We should be enjoying life in a grand way and allowing love to capture us! Does that mean we should sit idle? Does that mean we do nothing to gain that love? Of course not, we have a lot to do, but it does not involve a third party. It involves only you. The *whole, complete* and *happy* you. Many of us are walking around living a complete lie. Pretending to be happy with ourselves but we truly are not. We try so hard to be what society views as normal for a woman over the age of thirty that we never give ourselves the time we need to work on our own demons. We push those things aside such as loving ourselves, taking care of ourselves and building our brands for ourselves and just run towards love, as though love is some type of illusion we may never catch.

Life does not began when you have lost the title of "Single." Life begins when you are happy with yourself. That does not mean you can never gain love because you are over thirty, it just means you still have time to work out who you are meant to be in this life and prepare to be the right person for someone else. Many of us think that we are the right person and how much more can we prepare. We began to think that something is wrong with us because we are in this season. I used to think that way too. I thought something was wrong with me because I still had that title of "Single" attached to me but, I felt as though I already had everything together and was ready to be somebody's someone. I felt like I was hidden and could not be seen by no one because my title never changed but everything else was changing around me. New job, college graduate, my own apartment, new car. Things were good! But I later learned that wasn't the case I was not hidden from anything. I have just been on "reserve." I had to understand that what I physically had; the cars the education and so forth will not play a role in what I desire. You may feel as I have that being on reserve feels like forever and does not feel like love will ever come. You may even feel that you are completely prepared as I did also. And, you may actually be. But, being prepared is not just about having a job, having a home, having financial stability. Being prepared means that what is on the inside is well taken care of also. We can have all the glitz and glamour, but if we are not happy with who we are eternally, that glitz and glamour will never make us happy. Nor will another human being. So, no, waiting is not as bad as it may seem. Waiting allows God to fix what is on the inside and then pair you up with his best and in the right time. If I would have gained God's best for me two years ago, we would be divorced today. Who wants to be another statistic? I did not know who I was two years ago. I was partying, drinking, sexually immoral, and my priorities were all tangled. Most of all, I was not happy with who I was inside. My soul was stripped. I was angry, frustrated and anxious. I lacked self-control. I wanted love, now! No matter who it came from, but most importantly I did not love ME. So, no, I was not ready to love someone the way we should and I did not have a solid foundation of principles on how I should be seen by a man or how I am supposed to be as a wife or a mother.

My mess would have just divided another family apart and as bad as it may feel to wait. I know it's for the best. So, here I am *waiting*, not idly, but actively. I know that the desires of my heart will be met and sometimes I do grow anxious and try to speed up the process, but it just does not work. I am still lead back to waiting and I'm ok with that. I know that this season of singleness will not last forever. So while I'm waiting I will grow in my walk with Jesus, I will work out my shortcomings, I will travel the world. I will love on my family and friends and I will continue to love on me. Who knows, while you are busy living and enjoying what God has given us, Mr. Right could be right around the corner.

> *"Do you not know that in a race all the runners run, but only one gets the prize? Run in such a way as to get the prize. Everyone who competes in the games goes into strict training. They do it to get the crown that will not last; but we do it to get a crown that will last forever. Therefore I do not run like a man running aimlessly; I do not fight like a man beating the air. No, I beat my body and make it my slave so that after I have preached to others, I myself will not be disqualified for the prize"* (1 Corinthians 9:24-27 NIV)

2

My Story

I do not think I have ever had a "real" boyfriend. Well, what is real considered by society's standards and traditions? I have had men around, but there was never any real commitment. I do not like to go around pointing fingers. This just is not what this book is about, but let's just say I have had one too many bad dealings when it came to love and relationships. Of course I was young and the majority of my flings (YES, flings because it definitely was not anything DEFINITE) were not looking for anything serious. A steady relationship was just unheard of, it seemed to be all for fun. That is how I remember many of my dating experiences. Just fun. I do not remember feeling protected, I do not remember feeling a sense of security. Now, many times I went along with the dating game because I thought I could change a person into seeing what I saw. But it did not quite work that way. The norm became frustrating to me.

Love in my eyes was not a game, it was not a test of survival and it was not meant to be conditional. But it was all of that. I can remember pouring out my heart to someone and they did not even acknowledge it. That just hurts. I became tired of the heartache and dark rooms. Barely eating and begging men to be with me. That is not who I saw in the mirror. I knew I was not a woman who allowed this world to tear her apart. But, that is who I had become. I cannot say that part of what I was feeling was not my fault. It was. I allowed my wants and needs to be pushed to the side just so I could say I had a man. I became so familiar with not gaining a commitment from these men that I settled for his type of love for me. Not the type of love as discussed in the bible. The love that does not love with conditions or convenience. It is unconditional. It's the kind of love that is kind and caring, that does not cheat and is loyal. That protects. The kind of love that is not self-seeking but selfless.

I had to do some reevaluating of myself. I had to give up everything I knew about the love I had been given over the years and recondition myself to gain the love that I wanted and needed. I do not think I had experienced true heartbreak until I knew the things I wanted from a relationship and I was not receiving it. My story is much like any other woman's "Love Story." I will not sugar coat it or place a cherry on top to make it look better than what it was. But, I will be brutally honest that it has not been pretty. I have always been a "love hard" type of woman. I wore my emotions on my sleeve and totally went with the flow of things. I was never demanding of the things I wanted and I was always willing to make ANYTHING work. As I reflect back on my past, the easy way to sum it up was that I wanted ANYBODY, not somebody. Any man that came along who was "Fine" and gave me a spackle of attention had me at "Hello." I did not care that much about how he treated me or how many times he cheated. I just wanted him around and would beg him to stay when he wanted to go. He was comforting in a strange way. Now, that does sound like it was all my fault and that I put myself in that position. I admit it, I did, but that was coming from a "girl" who did not recognize the type of relationship we should have. I was immature in my thinking that love was what I had encountered over the past years.

So now what? I am thirty-one and single. I have no biological children and I am of course feeling like a ticking time bomb. I get asked daily who he is, when will I meet him and, "You know, after a certain age having children is high risk." Yeah, I know all of that and as hurtful as it has been hearing those things, I have found contentment in my situation, and sadly to say, it did not come until now. It took me six years to *GET IT*. I cannot quite describe how it went, but what I can say is that one day I felt something come over me and I just stopped in my tracks.

I was feeling this guy and maybe he liked me too. But, there still was no commitment. When I asked where it was going, His reply was, "I'm not ready for all that." We were deeply involved emotionally and physically. I was in love with someone who had no purpose for me in their life. At one point I was so involved that his words meant nothing and that maybe later he would change his mind, if I did more. But I still felt empty, I was not gaining anything, but maybe a few hours with him that left me wanting more after he was gone.

I was growing tired, and day by day I could not handle it any longer. I wanted more. I wanted a relationship and one with purpose. My vision has always been married with children. I just did not want to "date" for fun. So, I pressed pause on my so called life and took a long hard look at my surroundings. I was not happy at all. Dating men with no purpose, giving my body to someone other than my one day husband and being filled with uncontrollable emotions was not "fun" to me anymore. I did not grow up like this. I had morals, I learned morals and my immoral behaviors led me to feel rejected, lonely and bitter. I decided to just give it all up. I needed to get back to my foundation. I was completely lost as a woman. Hurting and worrying about my future.

When I was younger, my mom always kept my brothers and I in church. Of course being seven or eight in the church really was not a breakthrough for me. I did not grasp what church was all about. I just remember being told I had to go. I would always hear people say how good this guy named "God" was and that you could gain peace through his son, Jesus Christ. It was not until I got older that I realized who this magnificent man was. It was odd to me because through my bad and good times this man, named Jesus, gave me peace and courage. He gave me solid ground to stand on. He gave me hope through his word. And most importantly he told me not to worry. My past is gone and he would renew me. Just repent.

> **25** *"Therefore I tell you do not worry about your life, what you will eat or drink; or about your body, what you will wear. Is not your life more important than food, and the body more important than clothes?* **26** *Look at the birds of the air; they do not sow or reap or store away in barn, and yet your heavenly Father feeds them. Are you not much more valuable than they?* **27** *Who of you by worrying can add a single hour to his life?* **28** *And why do you worry about clothes? See how the lilies of the field grow. They do not labor or spin.* **29** *Yet I tell you that not even Solomon in all his splendor was dressed like one of these.* **30** *If that is how God clothes the grass of the field, which here today and tomorrow is thrown into fire will he not much more clothe you, O you of little faith?* **31** *SO do not worry, saying, 'What shall we eat? Or 'What shall*

we drink?' or 'What shall we wear?' 32 For the pagans run after all these things, and your heavenly Father knows that you need them. 33 But seek first his kingdom and his righteousness, and all these things will be given to you as well. 34 Therefore do not worry about tomorrow, for tomorrow will worry about itself. Each day has enough trouble of its own." (Matthew 6:25-34 NIV)

That made so much sense to me realizing how my worrying would lead me nowhere. That is when I felt I wanted to stop with the life I was leading and start chasing what really mattered, the "Good News," the Gospel of Jesus Christ. I was very amped to learn about who Jesus Christ was and his ways. I wanted to be a better person because, for so many years, I was ripped apart by terrible relationships. I lost a lot of hope in my desire to gain love and I lost a lot of myself chasing it. I wanted to stop worrying about the when and how and start living today. I began to heal. I focused my attention on becoming content in my season and enjoying myself in the process of waiting.

Many people ask, "Well, what you are waiting for? Are you waiting on a man thinking he will fulfill the voids of your empty soul? WHAT ARE YOU WAITING FOR?" As discussed earlier, I am not waiting in the literal sense. I am actively pursuing me so that I can be in position for all of God's goodness. That way, when he leads me to a wonderful partner, I will be prepared to embrace it wholeheartedly. And, the only way to get in position and live fulfilled was to surrender my life to the Lord. I cannot change a person and the way that they feel, only Jesus can change them. So I began to allow Jesus to change ME. In Psalms 37:4 the bible says, *"Delight yourself in the LORD and he will give you the desires of your heart"* (NKJV). My desire was to get myself right and then all that other stuff would follow.

When I was dating these men I was focused on pleasing them, to get them to stick around. I yearned to be accepted by someone. I thought happiness was found through another person. These hopes and dreams and my way of thinking had to go. And I had to get back to what I truly desired: unconditional, attentive, sacred, defined love. And I did not want anything less. I wanted more than just a title or a walk down the aisle. So, I decided I will wait and in the process I would get to know ME. I knew this newfound journey would cost me everything that I knew before. But, I was not worried about giving that up. I just wanted something to change. I wanted to stop feeling defeated as a woman, giving my all and not receiving anything back. Nothing as small as love, the agape love that is talked about in the Bible that was given to so many of the women of the scriptures. I learned that in order to get that love I had to find it within myself first and that came with renewing my thinking. No one can complete me and my happiness is not dependent on rather you have someone or not. Happiness starts within. And if I do not have happiness within myself, then no one else would be able to make me happy. So, I am here, pretty much in a season of loneliness. It is very quiet but undistracted. A time for me to heal.

REFLECTION

You have heard my story. Now, I want you to write YOUR STORY. Where are you at this point in your life? How did you get there? Even if you are not content, what would make you content? Be real with yourself and search deeply. I do not want you to think about it, I just want you to write whatever comes to mind.

3

Overcoming the Pressures of the World

Now you have written out your story and maybe you have reflected on your past and are surprised by what you wrote and how you got here. By now, you are probably wondering how your story ties into living a fulfilled life while being single. Well, before I could be at a place of contentment I had to reflect on the past to see the many things I may had done wrong and pick the learning experiences out of it. There is always a reason to grow and if you find no reason to grow you will be the same person forever, without any true success. Your reflections move you from point A to point B, without you even realizing it. You have probably never really thought about your story and how you got to this point, until now. Until someone was there to tell you to find the lesson so you can move forward.

So, now you have found the lesson, but one thing still remains, you are still single and are still having a slight feeling of discontentment. There are so many people around you who may be getting married and having children and even asking you every second of the day about your personal life—when, where and how you will have children and settle down and finally get married. People may even be thinking that something is wrong with you or they just think you are giving up on the idea of getting married and having children. Whatever, the thoughts or talk is about you should be none of *your* business. Honey, do not allow your discontentment come from the pressures of this world. We have enough to "think" about and worrying about the world and its views of us being single women over the age of thirty should be the last thing that is keeping you from living a fulfilled life.

Let me tell you about Hannah. Hannah is well known in the bible as a woman of great faith, she had great communion with the Lord. Any trouble she had she took it to him. She was devoted, godly and trusting unto the Lord. She allowed people to say hurtful things to her and instead of lashing out she placed those people in the Lord's hands. Hannah was the wife to Elkanah (who had another wife Peninnah. In those times having two wives was rather common). Hannah was barren and very pitiful and she could not bear Elkanah a son. In spite of all this she had an unblemished character. Through her struggle of not being able to bear a child, she never turned her back on God. She was still a praying woman. Peninnah, Elkanah's other wife, had many children by Elkanah and would provoke Hannah each time she went up to the house. She would irritate her until Hannah wept. Peninnah flaunted her accomplishment of having Elkanah's children and would tease Hannah for being barren. Elkanah loved Hannah very much and did not hold it against Hannah for not bearing him a son.

"Once when they had finished eating and drinking in Shiloh, Hannah stood up. Now Eli the priest was sitting on a chair by the doorpost of the Lord's temple. In bitterness of soul Hannah wept much and prayed

to the Lord. "O Lord Almighty, if you will only look upon your servant's misery and remember me, and not forget your servant but give her a son, then I will give him to the Lord for all the days of his life and no razor will ever be used on his head" As she kept on praying to the Lord, Eli observed her mouth. Hannah was praying in her heart, and her lips were moving but her voice was not heard. Eli thought she was drunk and said to her, "How long will you keep on getting drunk? Get rid of your wine" "Not so, my lord," Hannah replied, "I am a woman who is deeply troubled. I have not been drinking wine or beer; I was pouring out my soul to the Lord". (1 Samuel 1:9-15 NIV)

As you just read, Hannah was being provoked and talked about. This story hits home for me. We encounter so many pressures when we are not conforming to the world that we may want to act out of character, but that is not the proper way to handle things. You just have to come to a point in life where you tell everyone one else to BE SILENT and let you handle your own life. You must do as Hannah did and pour your cares onto the Lord and let it be. We can get so anxious that sometimes we may pressure ourselves and allow everyone else's opinion to negatively affect the outcome of our lives. Negativity can make or break you. If you believe that it will not happen then it will not happen. You must believe that you will gain the desires of your heart.

You have to fully become comfortable in your season. It is hard for sure. But, with some hard work on yourself you will have it under control. You see, it took me a very long time to get to a place of contentment and block out the loudness of the world. As a matter of fact it took me a very long time to stop messing around with my emotions by keeping doors open that should have been closed. I was getting blindsided by everything in life. I was a completely unstable woman conforming to how the world and men wanted me to be. I needed to rebuild my mind, body and soul from scratch and close out everyone else's views of where I should be in this life. I found that until I truly changed my mind, my life would not change.

Conformity is a disease within itself. It strips you of your own thoughts, wants and needs and you conform to the thoughts, wants and needs of someone else. Many times we submit to people and allow them to run our lives and at the end of it all we regret the things that we left undone. Instead of submitting my life to people (which I have done for many years) I submitted myself to Christ. My heart was being tugged, but I had one foot in the door of the kingdom and one out in the world getting ripped apart. I tried it my way for so long that it was time for a change. And, I knew that I wanted to please no one in this world more than I wanted to please Jesus, the one who died for me. I began to read my bible more, which gave me a new sense of hope. I began to serve in church more often which made me feel validated and I began to write this book which I never thought I could.

In my previous years I was so distracted by my addictions to walk how others wanted me to walk that I could not fully walk the way I was built to walk. I felt a true change in myself when I stopped caring about the world and its thoughts on who I was supposed to be at thirty-one or what I am supposed to have and I started caring about myself and loving myself. The pressure was lifted. I wanted to enjoy life and I could not enjoy life moping about my future (enough people did that for me). I had to STOP and think for myself. I cannot tell you how to get to that point, but what I will say is that you need to start living and not just existing in this life. You have to ask yourself who you are truly living for?

Each of us was uniquely created for our own destinies and when we began to live out other people's destiny we gave up on the life that was created for us to live. How could you possibly live fulfilled if you are constantly wearing the weight of the world on your shoulders? Every day you hear about another untimely death that has taken place. Can you imagine not waking up tomorrow and when you got to heaven you start to regret the things you could not do on earth that you were placed here to do. You could not fulfill your purpose because you were to be busy looking, watching, gawking the growth or non-growth of someone else's grass. I could not imagine it and it frightens me that if I left this world today I will not have served God by bringing people with me to the kingdom. I would not be too happy about it because I had spent majority of my life following someone else's footsteps instead of making my own tracks.

Do not allow the pressures of this world to detour you from the path you were set on to travel.

REFLECTION

What are some of the things you are hearing from people that is making you feel rushed?

4

The Art of Letting Go

I have had my number of bad relationships, mainly because none of them were "ready" to commit to me. After getting out my last relationship. I needed to get back to a level ground. I needed to Heal. It was a very devastating time because yet once again I failed at love. I needed space from men in general. So after the pieces were broken I kept to myself, closed off and not open to anybody. My mind was extremely messy and my heart felt like it would never beat again. Everything moved in slow motion, I did not want to go to work and when I did I cried ALL DAY. I did not want to eat or could not sleep. I remember one night I was crying myself to sleep as usual. The blinds were pulled tightly closed so no light would seep through, the lights were completely out and there was nothing but silence and darkness. As one tear after another hit my pillow all I could think about was all the hurt that I was feeling and how badly I wanted him back. No matter how much he showed me he did not want me or did not love me. My soul wanted him back. Months went by and I still would do the same thing. The stabbing pain I felt did not mean anything I was immune to the pain and I knew the only way to stop it was to get him back to me. I felt depressed at times and felt angry at others. I just could not get a grip on my emotions. It was terrible. My life was slipping away and I was allowing it to. I just could not let it go and untie my soul.

That my friends is what we call a soul tie. I was still holding onto the pain of someone who had already let me go. And I was not ready to move past it. I locked myself away and disappeared from the world, all over a broken heart and a tied soul. Instead of running away from the behavior I ran towards it. Our souls were connected spiritually and although he had released me and moved on I had not released him.

Soul ties are those ties you gain through spiritual connection. Soul ties are formed when the two people become one flesh. I had no idea that I was forming a soul tie with a man that had no intention on being my husband until I faced my heartache and still could not figure out why I was unable to let go. My soul was tied and it needed to be released. When I finally came to terms with all of this, I had to begin the healing process. It was not an easy process because before you can heal you have to suffer. It is much like a cut you get, it burns, stings and bleeds for a while. Days go by and it still hurts, but you do not feel as bad as the initial day you got injured. Your cut is now wrapped in a bandage, you cannot see it but you know it is there. Eventually there is no blood due to the pressure you applied to covering it up. The cut starts to form a new layer of skin and eventually turns into a scab. After weeks of nurturing that cut, the scab falls off and new skin takes the place of the wounded area. That is the healing process. You have to endure some suffering before it completely heals. You cannot focus on healing, you just have to focus on living and the healing will come. Now, what if after the scab appeared, instead of just focusing on other things and let it fall off on its own you focused on the scab. You continually picked at it and picked at it until you have picked the cut back open and it started bleeding again. How can you heal if you are continually focusing on what is hurting you? You have to let it go and untie your soul.

The art of letting go is not an easy task. It takes dedication and the "want" to get better. We become so desensitized to hurting ourselves that hurting ourselves does not seem like pain at all. I want you to think back to your last relationship or any relationship you have had in the past that you are not completely healed from. What is holding you back from healing? Do you know how to heal? Are you holding on to items that a past love gave you? Are you angry with them? Are you always on social media checking up on them? Have you completely given that area over to God and stopped focusing on it? Or are you sitting stagnant as I did and allowed my pain to overtake me? I searched every avenue to heal me and cover up the pain I was feeling inside. I tried anxiety medications, drinking, and partying. Those things relieved my pain temporarily, but I still was not happy and the depression became unbearable. I started journaling to let out excess frustration and I started to exercise to take my mind off of the pain I was still feeling. I even tried to get into new relationships, but the excess baggage flowed over into the new dating prospects. My heart was empty and my soul was ruined. I just did not want to bring myself to terms with letting go. It took me months; maybe even a year to finally accept it. I was tired. It was time to move forward. I began to clear out my closet as they say. I got rid of all the baggage from my past, anything that reminded me of that horrible relationship and I let it go. I made up in my mind that I did not want to live in a state of depression any longer and did not want the negative feelings toward love.

No one can tell you when to start healing and let go, that comes with some soul searching and much praying. But I will tell you, continually staying stuck in those feelings will lead you to a place called *NOWHERE*. Those negative feelings will never go anywhere unless you make them. You have to focus those negative feelings onto something positive. For me I knew I wanted to feel good about myself again. All that hurt and pain made me feel ugly on the inside and that ugliness seeped out my pores onto the outside. I was meaner, bitter and I was extremely closed off to the world. At thirty we do not have much time to spend on crying, wondering, wishing, chasing, begging, pleading and more importantly we do not have time to continue living in the past. God wants a newness for all of us and if we are to get this newness we cannot allow our past to dictate our lives.

I placed my cares on the Lord and, as odd as it may sound, I surrendered myself to allow a healing to take place. If we want to accomplish everything in life that we are meant to accomplish we cannot let a broken heart stand in our way. Yes, we will hurt, as a matter of fact, you may become brokenhearted once more but if you do; IF WE DO, this time you will be stronger to fight through the pain.

> *"Character is never built while standing in the pain; Character is only built while walking through the pain."* - Crystal Hall.

So I challenge you to unload all that hurt and heartache onto some paper, on a punching bag, on the pavement along the river and onto the Lord. Just as we take care of the outside of our bodies. We must take care of the inside as well. There is nothing like having inner peace and that peace comes when you have exhausted all possibilities of fighting against having it. We need God to fix our hearts before we can move forward to living how God envisioned us to live as his children. Holding on to the past is a death sentence killing our future. If we do not understand who we are and be confident in it, then we will never excel to the next level of our lives. If we do not make a commitment to ourselves to let go of the pain we will become bitter, meaner, uglier women on the inside that no one would want to be around. You may think you closed yourself off from the world while you are broken hearted, but imagine being shunned from the world when you are happy and whole. Not a good feeling, right? So unclench your hands and release all that pain.

If you are up for the challenge to change your hearts and release all that is in your hands, then the next aircraft is landing your way and this time your "carry-on" bag can be checked in at the counter! You are walking into a new destiny. And it is called Freedom!

REFLECTION

Use this page to UNPACK. Leave it all here. Let it all go!

5

Standards: Got Some?

As a single woman of course I have a "List." My pros, cons, things I'll compromise on, and those things that I will not. This list is not meant to be a part of that silly timeline us women know we have. Throw that list away because we know that life never sticks to timelines and things can happen out of order, changing at any given moment. The order is all linked to our divine purposes and we do not want to screw up a good thing by having some silly timeline in place. However, this list is only a list of characteristics you want from that "right" person. I look at it as a guideline to creating the life you deserve. We all know that when we get involved with another person who they are is who we have to accept. But, with a guideline full of characteristics of who the right person should be will allow you to either move forward or not. A list saves a lot of unnecessary drama. Of course I am not saying that your list is a list of perfection because we know NO ONE is perfect. But, we also know that we should be dealing with someone who brings out the best in us. Someone who pushes us toward success. Not someone who drags us down and belittles our character. This list should be about those characteristics that God wants each and every one of us to portray. This is not a list just about your "potential mate". It is also a list about us. That is why it is so important to get YOU right before trying to attract the right person.

Remember your potential mate will only be a reflection of who you are and where you are in your life. If you are empty, you will attract an empty man. God wants us to have his best son but, when we are empty and bitter God will not lead us to his best to only taint what he worked so hard to build back up. The mirror will just get turned on you, and we all know we hate looking at an ugly soul. I want you to also understand that your mate will not have every quality on your list. You may want things like tall, dark and handsome but, what if he is not exactly what you envisioned but he treats you as God wants a man to treat his wife? That is where you will have to compromise and figure out what is most important to you. I know you just cringed at the words "compromise" and "settle." Many people do not realize that compromise and settling have related meanings. It is just that people have used that word settling in such a derogatory and shameful way that people think it is some type of bad thing. People have taken the word "settle" which means "to adopt a new way of living; to come to an agreement," and have used it as a word that means to just give up and in to anything. Compromise, on the other hand, as defined in the Merriam-Webster dictionary means "to find or follow a way between extremes; to come to an agreement by mutual concessions." Both words are synonyms to each other. With both you are making an agreement to yourself that you will accept this "thing" for what it is. Do not think of accepting in a negative light, it just simply means you are willingly giving your consent to welcoming it with open arms and possibilities. I once heard a friend say that in every decision there could be a great outcome, it is just how you view it. You can either learn something from it or it could be the biggest life changer ever. Those compromises are those things that only you know will work for you.

I wrote a list about a year or so ago when I was at a point in my life where I was preparing myself to heal. My List looked like this.

1. Nice
2. Loyal
3. Nice looking
4. Wants kids
5. Loving

A very general list, right? I was writing it at a time of my anguish and emptiness. I knew generally what I wanted but it was not specific on things I needed and I knew God wanted for my life. When you are considering a mate you want to be sure of that person. It is not just about the feeling that person gives you but it is also about the PERSON itself. At that time I was looking for the "RIGHT ONE," the one that would treat me different than all the others. The one that made me feel different. I spent so much time on the feeling of how the RIGHT ONE would feel that I did not even consider the PERSON he should be. We do that. We get so hung up over our feelings and emotions that the "Person" does not exist. Anybody can make you feel good and wag their tongues to make what they are saying sound good. But, it takes a special *PERSON* to show with their actions how they are built in their soul and that is the person you want. The man who shows me that he will take God's instructions on how a man should treat his wife is the man I want. Not the man that shows me that my body means more to him than presenting me spotless and blameless. When I developed my "now list" I had to search deep. I knew that the person I wanted to be with had to be extraordinary. I knew that the person God needed for my life he would lead me to him, but he would not be the ordinary man I listed above. He had to be different because I am a different person now. What he was bringing to the table as far as material things did not matter. His character matters more.

For many years I was drawn to the "baller," the "fine" man, the "O Wee his body is tight and Right" man. His character never took precedence over his looks. Until I realized that one day those looks will fade and when they do, will I be happy with him as a person? If he had all the money in the world but treated me like crap would I be happy with that? If he had no vision for his life; would I be happy? If he did not love God, would I be okay with that? If he continually lied and cheated on me, would I be okay with that? Of course not! So, I had to dig and truly think about who I needed this man to be. The best way I found out who this man needed to be was in the bible. For many years I believed God would send me the Right One. The man that was specifically made for me. Just as Eve for Adam. But then a question formed in my mind. If Eve was the right one for Adam then how did Adam know that Eve was the right one? Simple: It was not because God told Adam she was. It was because Eve possessed the qualities that God instilled in her which made Adam realize she was that person. So what am I saying? God does not send us the Right One, he wants us to find the Right person who lines up with his word. Does this person lie? Is he a sluggard? Does he have discernment and self-control? Does he want to be a husband? Is he presenting you without blemish? Does he let God lead him or man (meaning popular television and our society)? Does he have a flattering tongue? **Get my point.** Those are the questions you have to ask yourself while writing your list. Does his character line up with the word of God?

Now ask yourselves, does your character line up with the word of God? Yes, we are listing qualifications that we hope our mates have, but we should also be considering that this list is a mirrored reflection of us. We are what we attract. Do you have the characteristics of who he should be lead to? Are you a Godly woman? Can you be a faithful wife? Do you have a harsh tongue? Are you loving? Are you a helpmeet? Do you possess any of the qualities of a Proverbs 31 woman? Did you know that in the book of proverbs men are provided with the characteristics of the right woman he should pursue and the woman he should stay clear of? The last chapter in the book of Proverbs is a chapter that every woman should strive to embody. This woman is virtuous; she is a woman who loves God, who respects her husband, who teaches her children, who is a helpmeet and submissive, who has self-control and is wise. She gives her life as a service to others, she cares for her body and she has an aura of peace and joy. Can you honestly say you possess those traits of a woman a man should be drawn too? So, as we see that it just is not about a list of qualities he should possess. While you are writing to attract a kingdom man you should be making sure you are a kingdom woman.

"A wife of noble character who can find? She is worth far more than rubies. Her husband has full confidence in her and lacks nothing of value" (Proverbs 31:10-11, NIV)

REFLECTION

Here is a blank page so that you can began your "LIST." Remember, make sure you leave a column available to check off each quality he should possess that you already have.

6

Dating vs Courting

There is a lot of talk going around about Dating vs Courting, the differences, the do's and do not's, and if you should or should not date at all, and just court. So, if you are all fixed up and ready to get back out in this dating world let's take a deeper look at both and gain a better understanding of both of these ways of getting into marriage. For thirty-one years I have dated, well the worldly definition of dating. I have created soul ties with men that I am no longer with that has hindered my progress in moving forward and developing a great relationship with another. For thirty-one years I have done the same thing when it came to dating. Not being fully committed to men but giving my body to them. Not being fully committed to a man but giving my heart to him. Not being fully committed to a man but sharing my soul with him. I have done it my way for thirty-one years and ended up with nothing but a broken spirit and empty soul. I have dated men instead of allowing myself to be courted by them. Being dated by men that sought after nothing more than the pleasure of being with me. The focus was more on chemistry instead of commitment, lust instead of purity. The dating relationships I have encountered was strictly driven by sex. We went out to the movies and out to restaurants and maybe dancing here and there but, it always ended up intimately. There was never a focus, it was always "go with the flow" and if it goes beyond that then we would discuss it when we got there. And of course it never got there.

In my dating relationships we never focused on the future. We lived in the moment. If we both were available we would "hook up" with no sense of urgency to move things along in a committed way. Our families were not involved at any point and the talk about commitment was scarce. I would say dating in my eyes was not purposeful. I always felt empty because I knew deep down that the men I was dating were only going to be around when it was convenient. I was always just an option, not a priority. Does this sound much like what you have gone through while "dating" a man? No focus, no commitment, no dream? Well that my sisters is what we call DATING in worldly terms. Now I know it sounds so bad. And you are feeling empty. But, how we approach relationships from now on can be turned around and those feelings will cease if we change the way we approach "dating."

Truthfully, I have never been one for dating anyway. I felt that creating a lot of soul ties with multiple people would lead me down a road I did not want to go. People would say, "Well, a free meal is always good, and the company is always better," but my sanity and focus for real love was more important than some free meal. So I scratched every thought I had about dating and renewed my mind with what I truly wanted and that was a Godly relationship where it had Purpose and Focus (*hence that is where my "List" came into play*). Not only did I want to save my body for my one day husband but, I wanted to get to know him without the emotional attachment of intimacy. I wanted to see if our interests would mesh well together; if what we could build could start as a friendship and progress into a courtship. I wanted to see if his focus for relationships were about pleasure and the moments or was it about purity and a lifetime. I wanted to know who was leading his life and would he be able to lead mine. I wanted, for once in my life, this man to feel good about me without taking off my clothes.

We all have dreams of how we want our relationships to go, but the relationship cannot go anywhere if the "person" and focus is not right. I wanted to figure out how to better approach "dating" without all the other stuff. How could I have a meaningful relationship where both goals were moving toward marriage? So, by now you may be asking, "What is courtship?" The Collins English dictionary states that courtship "is the act, period, or art of seeking the love of someone with the intent to marry." That is how I view my relationships where the focus is on developing a relationship that will lead to marriage. Courtship in my opinion does not involve the same emotional attachment that comes when you are in a casual dating relationship. Your focus is on that person and building a future with them. If you can think back to your relationships, what was the foundation? I know many of my relationships were merely based on emotional attachments which came from intimate situations. I was never allowed the chance to build memorable moments with my then partner.

The goal of our dating relationship was to have fun. My emotional attachments led me to be blinded by feelings instead of thinking if this PERSON is the right person for me. We never got out of our comfort zones with one another. We were just comfortable. I was willing to date ANYBODY no matter what was in their spirit. I never sought counsel while dating and my family and friends was not there to help me through the process. I knew I wanted Marriage to be my end result and I thought by casually dating, it would lead me there. I often thought about how my dating life would have been different if no intimacy was involved in the situation and I was just able to get to know the person. Example: I love chocolate ice cream. If I had never tasted chocolate ice cream would I love it as much as I do? Probably not. What I am getting at is that if we did not date the way we do would we be as emotionally unstable as we are? Something to think about. Right?

It is very easy to approach dating in the worldly view. Because everyone is afraid of rejection so they sought after many people at one time and choose when they are ready to settle down. But, that is not the way to go. When you have many spirits around you, you lose your focus and those spirits can make you become confused of your clear view of the things you want and do not want. I know it sounds boring and it might even sound lonely. Who wants to just court one person when there are thousands out here, but then you have to ask yourself are you going to marry all those people. Or, are you trying to create the perfect person by dating all those people. What I am trying to get you to see is that dating in the worldly view leads to lack of commitment and confusion. Whereas courting has a specific goal attached to it and if you do not want to move in that direction with another person then you sit still and wait for the person who gives you all of what you desire and who will show you those qualities that God wants every one of us to entail.

Every courtship is different but the goal is the same. Each couple has its own guidelines while courting. Some courting relationships are done in private but most are public. Families are involved, friends are involved and the focus of the relationship is centered on Godly principles. Back in the 1800's courting was the formal manner in which relationships developed. Courting back in those times was a way for the parents to do all the work required to get their children prepared for marriage. Young women learned culinary skills and how to become a good mother while young men learned how to become chivalrous and responsible. Marriage rings were then introduced as a formal way of asking the parents' permission to have their daughters hand in marriage. The children could not be alone together and there was definitely no intimacy. All social activities were done under supervision. These social activities showed the development in the relationship and if the relationship mashed well. The social activities consisted of those activities that interested both individuals. Families were very involved in the courtship of their children. Their role helped identify those characteristics and traits of a potential partner. It was not unheard of that many of the older women played match makers to find suitable mates for the younger women. Not like in today's dating world, there is no romance, no adventure, no focus and no family.

That way of "courtship" reminded me of the story of Ruth and Boaz in the bible. This is the perfect story of how influential families were in the courtship of their relatives or even non-relatives. Ruth's story started off by showing her dedication to serving people while she was suffering through her own pain and turmoil. When she became a widow she made a vow to help her elderly mother-in-law after the death of her husband as well. And in return her mother-in-law used her wisdom to find a suitable mate for Ruth to fulfill the purpose of God's plan. This story of Ruth and Boaz shows misfortune with love, loyalty and then the ultimate reward for following the instructions of a much older and wiser woman. Ruth then became one of the most prominent women in the bible and the great grandmother of Israel's great king David. So, now we see that family is so important when it comes to courting. Your family will play the role by keeping you focused in your courtship and will also help you distinguish the right person from the wrong one.

Courting like this is truly unheard of in our day. It is one of those things I believe people are afraid to do because no one wants to give up their "freedom" card. The joy of "dating" many people at once kept them happy. Many people want to continue to just let things flow until someone at some point gets tired and leaves the situation. But the majority of the time that just does not happen and we just do not get tired. We get comfortable and frustrated, blaming the other person for our own unhappiness because we were not willing to say, "Enough is enough," and leave those "relationships" that were not meaningful and taking up time that could be given to someone who truly cares. I believe many times we become okay with the "status quo" and at the same time become bitter because of our own actions that, in the end, were preventable. So what now?

My feelings are that in order to change our situations we must approach things differently. Our minds must be focused on doing it the right way. We need to take ourselves from being complacent and put ourselves in the place of completeness. Being happy and whole women in healthy and whole relationships. Courting, I believe, is one of the ways to approaching meaningful relationships. Courting will eliminate half, if not more, of the drama, heartache and time given to relationships that are not meant for us to be in. Our focus must be on approaching these situations in realistic and healthy ways, using the characteristics and principles that God gives us freely about who the "right" person should be. Here are a few of those traits or principles you should ask yourself while in the courtship.

1. Is he a prudent husband? Does he have self-control and discernment?
2. Is he a liar or someone with a flattering tongue? In the book of Proverbs theme is wisdom and it states that "a lying tongue hates those it hurts, and a flattering mouth works ruin" (Proverbs 26:28). Does he use his tongue to get what he wants and after he gets it, do he go back to his defiled character?
3. Is he loyal, is he a cheater?
4. Is he a sluggard?
5. Does he present you spotless and blameless?
6. Is he always trying to get in your bed instead of your heart?
7. Is he dating multiple women? Or better yet, does he want to just date multiple women and figure out who he wants?
8. What are his motives?

These are just a few questions you need to consider before starting a courtship. But even through courting you need to work on becoming the right person as discussed in the earlier chapter. Ask yourself, "Do I have self-control? Do I have a flattering tongue or loose lips? Do I put down others? Will I be a helpmeet or a nightmare?" It says it in the word, "Better to live on a corner of the roof than share a house with a quarrelsome wife" (Proverbs 25:24 NIV), with quarrelsome meaning argumentative. Will you be a woman of noble character or one that loves to nag about everything? Will you pick your battles or let your battles pick you. You must be prepared for a courtship because it is a huge decision with the ultimate outcome of marriage, something we women dream of. I had to understand what I wanted in order to get to this place of me not wanting to date any longer. I was looking for something more and I knew I could not find it dating many people. So I decided to put myself on reserve for the one who will court me. Who will show me FIRST that courting is what he wants to do from the beginning. He would have to show me that he is more interested in my life than just the pleasure we could possibly give one another. We need to see if we fit and if he would be able to lead the relationship, not by the physical but by the spiritual.

There is always a right and "not so right" way to do things. One way could lead to a lifetime of bliss and the other could lead you back to a road of heartache and constant soul ties. I do not know about you but, my end result will be marrying the person whom God sees fit for my life. And I can only make God proud and myself whole by approaching the relationship in a godly way.

REFLECTION

Your OWN definition of Dating?

Your OWN definition of Courting?

What will be different next time around?

7

Me Time

I had just arrived back in Detroit, MI about an hour before and I was completely exhausted. I drove four hours headed north to a city in Michigan called Traverse City. It was just me and the road; much needed "me" time. I had never been to Traverse City and it was on my list of things *To Do* this year (every year I create a sort of Bucket List of things to do). I had always heard how beautiful Traverse City was and so I decided to take a few extra days off work and explore. Before I made any plans I was not sure if I would go in the first place (I had no one to accompany me on this trip) but, I took a chance and decided to just live for once. It had been many months that I had planned to go anywhere and I did not want to miss another opportunity to travel and see places I had always wanted to see. So I packed my bags and started driving. Needless to say I had a great time! I arrived in Traverse City four hours later after leaving Detroit at eleven that morning. The weather was beautiful and the city itself was breathtaking. Traverse City is surrounded by the moderating effects of Lake Michigan and is considered the largest producer of tart cherries in the United States. Traverse City features freshwater beaches, the sleeping bear dune trails, and a National lakeshore. Many festivals such as the film festival in the park, cherry festival and wine and cheese festival are some of the most known events to partake in. I have a "go-getter" type of personality when it comes to life.

I love to see and do new things. Although I do not always have the people around to accompany me, I still like to go.

Imagine standing on the beach and watching the sunset. The sun is glistening as it descends into the clouds but, it stops before it completely lowers. As though it were stopping to smile at you (that is just how bright the sun illuminated from the sky). I felt something so peaceful and calm come through me. It was the most beautiful sunset I ever watched in my life. And it was just hours from my hometown. Now ask yourself, why would we want to miss opportunities like this? Is it because we do not have the time, or we do not have anyone to share those moments with, or we are afraid of sitting with ourselves and afraid of what emotions may come out? Life is about capturing the beauty of every moment. If you sit and wait on the side of the rode too long and watch all the buses go by and do not stop one of them, you may actually be missing the bus of a lifetime.

With the weight of the world on our shoulders as women; we need to take some time out just for "me." We think too much, we wait too much and we look too much. Before you know it all that thinking, waiting and looking will be the obstacle in the road stopping us from passing by. Many times we feel guilty about having "me" time. We feel guilty about spending our hard earned money on ourselves because we are such big givers. But, in order to get that love you want you must treat YOU the way you want others to treat you. You can still give your time to others but, sometimes you need to just give your time to yourself; get to know who you are, the things you like and what you dislike. Those wants and needs you want from your one day spouse starts with knowing who you are first.

My time is very limited, I am a very involved aunt to a three-year-old and with all his activities (that I want to get him involved in) and family things it seems like I have no time just for ME. I have work obligations and plus, I try and get very involved at my church (where would I find the time to write this book, would you not like to know). So time escapes me many times. Not to mention finances do not always add up and I do not always have the girlfriends to do things with, so I sometimes feel held back even more to do the things I like to do. But, where there is a will there is a way! I stopped making excuses and started just doing. I make sure I make time for ME and I no longer feel guilty about it. I do not want to be the old, mean woman who stays away from people because I am mad at myself for not living my life. Nor do I not want to be that mother that live vicariously through their children's lives. I want to live my life and then have many stories to tell. So, no I do not feel guilty about taking time for me. If I did I would have never started this book. I would never understand who I am and who I am meant to be if I did not have that quiet time to myself. It is easier said than done but it is required!

For single moms, I understand your kids have obligations and you have obligations to your children. However, what child likes a parent that lacks sleep, quiet time or just that breathing space. Without it you become mean, overbearing, angry and sometimes even depressed and your children could suffer even more than they would suffer for a few hours without you. Get out and set some time aside just for YOU! You do not even need your girlfriends around, this time should be just for you to have a good time alone and learning yourself. Now, I know some of you have read that sentence and said "NO FRIENDS!" Oh no, does she mean cut my friends off? OF COURESE NOT, you need confidants and people around but, what I do mean is get to a place where if your friends cannot go with you to the places you are dreaming of going become comfortable with going alone. At the end of the day who is the person you still have to live with no matter what? That is correct, YOU. So start taking care of yourself.

I would consider myself a loner; I mean I love for others to be around but, I do not have any issue with being with myself. Going to restaurants, the movies or even traveling by myself are not a problem. I am very comfortable with an empty space. I live for those moments where I can take a few hours to just sit with myself and learn me. Reading my bible, talking and hearing from God is a treasure. It was not easy though, at one time I feared being alone because of emotions I had buried inside. I was afraid to confront my emotions. Until I confronted my feelings and got rid of them, focusing on my emotions was how I spent my time. I had to deal with my loneliness. So, I invited every emotion I had inside in. If I wanted to cry in my quiet time, I cried. If I wondered "Why," I asked and if I wanted to scream, I screamed. I understand not everyone is like me but, understand that having ME time is required for a healthy lifestyle. Emotions cannot be suppressed they have to be dealt with and if you do not deal with them they come right back. As hard as it may seem, you just have to deal with it and then let it go. Fight through the pain and get to the other side where your power is. Do not allow the emotions to hold power over you. Control them. As soon as you do your ME time will be more enjoyable to you.

I am big on lists (as you can tell). I love creating them. It gives me a guideline on accomplishing goals. During some of my ME time, I grab my journal and just create goal lists. And I encourage you to do the same. These lists are of things you have always wanted to do and every time you accomplish something on the list check it off. It is quite exciting! How about I help you start the process?

Write your list. This list should be as long or as short as you want it to be. It should have places you want to go and things you want to see. This list should include strictly some ME time things, i.e., take a class at your local gym, go to the spa, take a day trip to a nearby state (for me it's Chicago, but there are some beautiful cities on the upper peninsula of Michigan that I would not mind visiting), treat yourself to dinner and a movie. Pick a quiet spot, your favorite beverage and just start writing. Do not think about your future thoughts just write, daydream and fantasize about those places you want to see and those things you want to do.

Do something you have always wanted to do. For me it was starting this book. I do not know how many times I put it on the back burner and how many lists I have created with "Write a book" on it before I actually did something about it. You have to create your life and your legacy. Working in corporate America is GREAT but, I know there is more to you than just corporate work. Have you always wanted to start a blog? Or have you wanted to sell jewelry? Make Clothes? Teach others? Utilize the talents that God has blessed you with or you will lose them. Serve in your church. Volunteer at a soup kitchen, do things that make you feel good.

Travel. Now I know this one may ruffle some feathers because the first thing that is on some minds are, Finances. If we keep saying what we do not have, we will never have it. Start getting creative with the finances you do have. There are a lot of great sites that hold travel deals daily. Do your research and you will find the deal of your life. The second thing that is mentioned is I have no one to travel with. Well there are sites that are strictly geared towards singles. They have singles cruises, singles retreats and much more. When it comes to traveling you have to get creative and stop allowing your current circumstance stop you. There are so many beautiful places to see. Get out there and broaden your horizons. Sometimes traveling does not mean you have to leave your own city. Be your own tourist. I am sure there are some beautiful things to see just around the corner from you. If you ever want to see some beautiful landmarks come to Detroit, we have a lot of great bed and breakfasts and spas. Treat yourself, Remember that is the name of the game.

Beyond ME time there is always get-to-know-your-family time. Family members will not always be around so, how about spending some time with your elderly family, especially if you still have living grandparents, aunts and uncles. Having family time is beautiful. The love you strive to gain from others you can get from your family. Did you know laughter is the way to healing a broken soul? Get around some family, pull out the old photo albums and watch how laughter and smiles fill the room. Reminiscing on childhood memories and just feeling that warmth you get from family is priceless. Make some more memories and take lots of pictures because one day the ones around you may not be there. Do not take this time for granted. Life is very short and if you do not start living it, that time will pass you by. We only get one try at life so utilize some of the time for yourself and the ones who are around you. Taking time out for you should always be a priority of course you will feel much more relaxed and energized.

I must admit I have a guilty pleasure and that is getting a pedicure. It is the little things that will make you feel confident inside. God did not create us so that we could not live life. God wants and needs for us to see his creation and live joyously. So, when you get off work and come home to plan your night and remember to include the most important person in it: YOU.

> *"I have come that they may have life, and that they may have it more abundantly" (John 10:10)*

REFLECTION

Use this page to start your "To-do List". Have fun with it ladies!

8

Trusting Your Season

"He has made everything beautiful in its time."
(Ecclesiastes 3:11)

You may now say that you are starting to feel better about being single and that things look very promising with your contentment. But, you still do not trust that you can come to terms with it. Everything sounds good on paper but, when it comes to the doing, you get stuck. You cannot began to even think of how to pick up the pieces and start fresh and trust that there is a time and place for everything. You cannot simply open your hands and just let go of that tight grip you have on control. You have let go of the past but you have yet to let go of the future and just go with the flow. You may even be attempting to fake this process and put makeup on a smile that really is not there. Believe me, I know it takes time and more books, coaching, reading, developing and learning to get to the place where you are renewed and believing that your time will come. This all is a test of *Faith*, a test to see if you can overcome and move forward to what is really destined to be yours. *FAITH* and *TRUST* are two very hard things to do. Especially when you cannot see what you are trusting in.

You may even have a hard time trusting yourself because those dark places are so comforting to you. Whatever the case may be you have to learn and train yourself to Trust your season. Stand firm in your Faith, trust that the Lord will give you the desires of your heart and believe that you will receive it. We cannot try and speed up the process, but as long as we know that without a doubt it will be, then there is no need to sit stagnant and wait. I know it seems hard to surrender yourself to an outcome you cannot see and it feels unsafe to move. But where is your Hope? We have all had times where we felt as though we had lost all hope in ourselves and in God. Believing that he will not work on our behalf. Losing your hope makes trusting our season a lot harder.

Let me ask you this: Did you ever trust a friend with a huge secret and knew they would not tell a soul? Or, did you ever have faith that you would get that job you wanted? And when you believed and did not sway from believing it to come true the outcome was just as you imagined it to be and more. Why is it so easy for us to trust and have faith in people but, have no trust and faith in ourselves? We do not trust ourselves enough to let go and let our faith carry us.

Seasons change quickly but, with every season comes a time for you to change. This season of singleness is the change you need. It is a time for you to grow beyond what you have ever known. It is a time to be renewed in your hearts and souls. Sometimes I feel we harden our hearts because of the pain that may have been inflicted on us in the past. We never give ourselves a chance to heal so, of course, we have a hard time trusting and having faith that we can get and have everything we deserve. This bond we have with distrust and lack of faith needs to end. We must break down those walls we have built and start being hopeful again. Anticipating the best, and trusting that when we come out of this season we will come out better than before.

Have you ever tried to chase after a fly and could not catch it. I mean you tried everything. Closing doors to barricade it in, turning off the lights so it would not see you coming towards it. Do you remember how irritated you were trying to catch that fly only to find out if you open the door the fly would fly out and you would be at peace again? That is much like what we do to ourselves when do not trust our season. If we would just open our minds and hearts and accept this season then we would see the benefit of it when we come out.

I can remember a time where I hated being in the season of loneliness. I wanted people around, particularly the men that I was dating. I was in a constant battle with myself to hold onto the things that were hurting me and I felt if I let them go I would be alone and I could not be alone. My battle was to either let go or hold on. It had become a true fight to let go. But, I knew it was for the best. I knew I would be a much better person after all the back and forth I had to endure. So, deciding to let go and trust my season was the best thing I could have ever done. It was not easy by far and there were days I could not stand to be by myself. But, those were the times I had the most success in my growth. There were times I fought with myself to try and go back to my past life but I had to adjust my thinking and figure out my motivation for doing this. Did I want to do it just because I was lonely or did I really want to become a better person and prepare myself for all the things I desired? I knew one thing, I did not want to be the messy woman anymore. The one with the emotional issues and ugly character.

This season has allowed me to crack open a shell that was so harden by the devastation of many relationships. It is so hard to be the only single girl sitting at a table full of married, engaged or courted women. However, it was a great learning tool. They all continue to inspire me in their own way. It gave me a sense of HOPE that although I did not know their full journey I knew it was possible to get that love that I desired. I gave congratulations and I truly felt happy for anyone who was standing where I wanted to be. Years ago I would not have been able to do that. But since I have grown in my faith and started to trust my season and use this time wisely while I am here. It has been the most amazing journey I have ever been on. Like it is stated in the bible there is a time and place for everything and one day it will be my time but, for now I am, *"Trusting and enjoying my season."*

Trust your season ladies. Let it surprise you and trust God's timing for he has his best waiting on you.

Do your Homework

There is a time and place for everything,
And a season for every activity
Under heaven:
A time to be born and a time to die,
A time to plant and a time to uproot,
A time to kill and a time to heal,
A time to tear down and a time to build,
A time to weep and a time to laugh,
A time to mourn and a time to dance,
A time to scatter stones and a time to gather them,
A time to embrace and a time to refrain,
A time to search and a time to give up,
A time to keep and a time to throw away,
A time to tear and a time to mend,
A time to be silent and a time to speak,
A time to love and a time to hate,

A time for war and a time for peace. (Ecclesiastes 3:8)

REFLECTIONS:

Do you trust your season? What are some of the things you want changed within yourself that you will benefit from and that will make you a better person?

9

Building Your Happiness

Coming to terms with your season is hard. It takes work. However, it is a beautiful season to be in. Your single season not only allows you to be free but, it also allows you to build a story of legacy for yourself. I know none of us like being single but, if we just learn to enjoy the NOW and not think about the future we can definitely build a castle of happiness while in this season, and know that things are made beautiful in due time. Think of a caterpillar, how could a caterpillar turn itself into a beautiful butterfly over the course of one season? Think about that process. A caterpillar makes its own shell forming it into a cocoon shape and on the inside it is transforming itself to become the beautiful creature we see today. That is amazing! And that is how we have to be. We have to take this single season and transform ourselves from the inside out. How can you know your purpose for life if you are so stuck on being single? What I have been trying to get you to see is that being single is not a deathly disease that is only giving you two days to live. Being single is the place where we are now and it does not have to last forever. It is all about creating your story and getting out there and living it.

Take risks and leaps and allow the waves of the ocean to carry you freely. Build your happiness. Do not allow what is around you to keep you from starting the foundation of who you will eventually become. Ladies, we have to get out of our own way to happiness. We have to stop allowing our emotions to dictate whether we are happy or not. We have to stop allowing our circumstances to dictate whether we can be happy without having someone by our side. Now, that is not to say that you should be this independent woman and do not need anybody for anything. But that is just to say that your happiness does not depend on anyone but you. There is so much to see in this lifetime, you do not have time to just sit around and be sad over small circumstances that you cannot change right at this moment. So what, you are in another wedding as a bride's maid; so what, you do not have a date to a concert. Go anyway and have a great time! Remember there are a ton of potentials around you but, you cannot see them because you are so busy turning up your nose at what other people have that you may feel like you are lacking. Baby, age is a number and that number should not make you feel less of a person or in any rush. We only get one life to live and if we are going through that life not seeing things, not doing anything, sitting on the sidelines waiting for our happiness to come then I think we may be waiting a long time.

Happiness is not something that is found or should be looked for, it is already within us. We just have to be willing to embrace what is there already. We have to learn that people will not make us happy. Eventually someone will do something you will not like and the happiness you think you found in that person will vanish. That is why it is so important to find happiness within ourselves and know that we can make ourselves happy. Clearing out your cluttered body and mind is a sure way to start embracing your happiness. Making that list of places and things you want to do is a sure way of embracing your happiness. It does not take much, it just takes you getting rid of all the negative feelings you have toward yourself and start treating yourself with respect and love. It will show when you start embracing your happiness, you will feel better, look better and want better for your life. People will start noticing your changes and they will start telling you how happy you look, all because you are truly happy on the inside. Your season is no longer dictating who you are because you are embracing this time and enjoying every minute of it.

I watched some of my friends travel around the world with their significant others and wished to myself, how badly I want that and how tired I was of being single. I was acting as if my singleness was a bad spell that some witch had put on me and I could not get it off. I was always looking at someone else's grass instead of watering my own and making my own look like something beautiful. I was watching people be happy and I was not truly happy but, I wanted what they had and my happiness did not matter. But, it does matter. Being happy will get you those things you desire. So focus not on what is on the other side of the road. Focus on what is on your road.

It starts with speaking the right things.

"The tongue can bring death or life; those who love to talk will reap the consequences. (Proverbs 18:21 NIV)

"What goes into a man's mouth does not make him unclean but what comes out his mouth that is what makes him unclean" (Matthew 15:11 NIV)

This simply means that how you talk can predict what you will gain in your life. If you are constantly down on yourself and talking negatively toward yourself you will attract that same behavior. Yes, you are talking negatively to yourself when you say, "It is never going to happen," or "I'm too old," and "I'm not good enough," and, "I'll just give up on (insert negative speech here)." All those statements are negatively effecting your life and you cannot build your happiness with negative talk. Start talking yourself up. "I am happy." "I am worthy of all things." Start changing your perspective on life and watch life change for you.

> "Finally, brothers, whatever is true, whatever is noble, whatever is right, whatever is pure, whatever is lovely, whatever is admirable-if anything is excellent or praiseworthy-think about such things" (Philippians 4:8)

Building your happiness also starts with *thinking the right things*. This goes right alongside of speaking the right things. What a man thinks is what he will speak. We cannot force a thought out of our minds but, we can allow the thought to come, deal with it, replace it and then let it go. You have to get in the habit of not allowing your thoughts to control you. We have to watch what we see, be it on television, hearing songs on the radio and seeing it on social media. So, if you have to go unplugged for a day or a week or a month, whatever you desire, then you have to do it. Your mind needs to be reconditioned and you need to know that negative thoughts will come but you do not have to allow it to stay. You have to learn to deal and let it go.

Being happy also means *being content* with your portion. A lot of people get contentment mixed up with being complacent and lazy. Contentment does not mean you do not try and work hard to gain what you want. Contentment simply means you will leave the results up to God. You will go after those things you want but, you will be completely satisfied with what God gives you. We can act so ungrateful for the portions God has already given us that it is stripping us of having more of what we want. If we are always acting ungrateful for what we have now, then how can we really be grateful for the things to come? Start showing gratitude for your life now! Do you have a roof over your head? It may not be the grand home you want but it is a smaller version of it. Be content. Do you have food to eat? It may not be a filet mignon but a Delmonico is just as good. Be content. Do you have transportation? It may not be a luxury vehicle, but it runs properly and it is fairly new and gets you from point A to point B with no problems. Be content. Do you have your health? Are you exercising and eating right but still have a small health aliment like asthma. Be content. Do you have family and friends? You may not have many friends but all your immediate family is still living. Love on them and be content. Did God wake you up this morning? And yet, you are still complaining the sun is shining too bright into your window. Be content. All those things deserve your approval, it needs to be said that you are grateful for what you have now and that you are satisfied with the portions that God has given you. Show that you are content in your season of singleness and preparing yourself for the next phase of life. Showing that simply means get up with a smile on your face, feel it in your heart and when people ask about your singleness speak positive about it. Say something like, "It is coming and I haven't given up on it so while I'm waiting I'm enjoying my portion. I am so grateful for my life and what I have now." Talk yourself up to the point that you believe it in your soul.

Building your happiness simply means taking on the character of a truly happy person. God has given his grace for us to live joyfully. It is already been placed inside of us. We just have to embrace it. Take off that shield of worry and fear. Know that in just a blink of the eye you can gain all your heart's desires but first, you have to embrace your happiness and that starts within you.

> *"I know that there is nothing better for men than to be happy and do good while they live. That everyone may eat and drink, and find satisfaction in all his toil—this is the gift of God" Ecclesiastes 3:12-13 (NIV Bible)*

Reflections

"Exercise"

What are some things you are grateful for?

As you jot them down on this paper, take some post-it notes and start to place them on a gratitude board or on your bathroom mirror. Each morning get up and recite what you are grateful for. This is a sure way not to forget the things you already have that you could be taking for granted. (You will have additional space on the following page.)

Journaling Space:

10

Finding Your Purpose

At this time in life you may feel you have it all together but still may feel like something is missing. Of course the single thing is a missing link in the puzzle but, you are not feeling fulfilled either in life. You may hate your job and feel useless getting up every day dreading to go to some place that is not challenging you enough or that is not keeping your focused enough. You feel unhappy but, you still are grateful for having a job even if it is not your dream job. Now we are getting someplace—your dream job. We all have a purpose in this life and although you feel stuck at some job you feel is dead end, that job could be creating your purpose.

Many of us do not truly know our purpose or what makes us happy. For me, I always knew I wanted to help people. However, while I was a freshman in college I decided to get my undergraduate degree in Fashion Design. I loved clothes, loved making them but, I still did not feel fulfilled. Many times I became frustrated making clothes. It was so much detail and sitting at a sewing machine for hours was not my "dream job". Although I love fashion it was (and is) more of a hobby than what I wanted as a career. Beyond that, I did not want to move out of Michigan. So, I continued to search for purpose. I started to search for what I ABSOLUTELY loved to do. I remember as a young teenage girl I would gather the other little girls in my neighborhood and would act as though I was there teacher. We would choreograph dances together. I felt like I was to guide them in some way so I took them under my wing (because they were so much younger than I was).

I also remembered a time where I would line up my baby dolls and try and mimic my teachers in school. I would get a card board box and use that as a board and get some of my mom's old medical books and use those as my teaching materials. My mom would always tell me that I had the "gift to gab." I guess that meant I just had the gift of talking too much. Through many years and job changes it was always on my heart to just help people somewhat like a therapist but, I wanted to help women that identified with me. I wanted to be that person people came to and felt okay to talk with, even if it was just to listen to them and give a warm smile. So, where am I now? I landed a job far from the fashion industry. I manage staff and, guess what, the majority are women over the age of eighteen. You see each season in my life has prepared me for my purpose. Each job I had prepared me for who I am today. I never, in a million years, thought I would truly write a book to minister to women. Or to even tell my story. I guess when they say your life comes full circle it truly does. I LOVE helping people and helping them to change their lives by using the words given to me from God, to speak to them. Every job, every situation I have endured in my life has led me to this moment. I believe I have found purpose. For so many years I ran away from what I knew God placed on me to do. I remember going to a church and the pastor saying to me that I had such a fire inside of me and when it comes out life would be so different. I found my purpose when I submitted my life to Jesus and allowed him to use me for his glory.

At this point you may feel like you do not know your purpose and you are tired of the feelings of being unfulfilled. That is where you need to just surrender. God has already given you the plan for your life. But are you sensitive to it? What is the one thing that makes you feel so happy and fired up when you do it? That is your purpose. Think back to when you were a child and those things you did. Maybe you were playing an instrument and it just lit up a room. That is your purpose. We all are destined to be great people when we find our purpose and stop living aimlessly. Finding your purpose may seem like it will take a lifetime to do. However, your purpose has always been inside of you; you just have to uncover it. So let's talk about how to uncover your purpose.

God says, "For I know the plans I have for you, declares the Lord, plans to prosper you and not to harm you, plans to give hope and a future" (Jeremiah 29:11, NIV). God knows the plans for your life he has given you gifts that will prosper you and move you forward in ways unimaginable to the eye. It will feel like a sense of release. Now, I do not want you to think that I am saying quit your job and live carefree (if that is what you enjoy doing). What I am saying is that while God is getting you to your purpose you will still have to go through the steps to get to where he wants you to be. And when you get there you will understand why you had to go through those steps. You should look at every situation as a stepping stool to where you need to be. God puts us in places aligned with his plan so that we can gain the wisdom and learn the lessons from it.

I remember a friend telling me how bad her job was and that she did not feel that she belonged there because there was so much turmoil. She knew exactly what she wanted to do but she landed a job that went against her character. I just remember telling her that there may be a lesson in that job. Of course she could not see that because she was blinded by all the negativity that came with the job. Needless to say she is not at that job anymore but, she gained much knowledge to now start her own business, something she has wanted to do from the beginning but did not know how. Although it was painful to stay in that position she stayed there because she became sensitive to knowing how God was working in her favor. She even gained things that she always wanted to learn how to do but did not know where to start to learn how to do them. Now, starting her business she has the proper tools to move forward and the puzzle started to look a little more finished than before. She began her business plan, started a website and started writing proposals (something she wanted to learn and that job taught her how to do it). That is what it is all about, finding the lessons in every situation good or bad. God placed her in that position not to defile her but to uplift and push her forward on her path. Is that not beautiful how God can use situations to get you to where you need to be? We think that it is horrible while we are in it but, God just cannot wait to show his glory through it. From glory to glory. Amen!

So ladies that is what you have to do; you have to start opening your eyes and mind and be sensitive to God's direction. He has already given you the purpose. It is time to start getting busy and noticing your surroundings. Everything has its reason. So that dead end job you feel you have, try looking for the purpose in it. It is doing more than giving you the tools to move you forward. It is preparing you to walk in God's purpose for your life.

REFLECTION

What is your purpose?

Conclusion

I know this journey has not been an easy one. Reliving the past and disconnecting yourself with the future could be one of the hardest things you may endure. But, the best part about this is you have overcome your singleness. This book is no magic tool to get you a man quickly, but it is a great tool to start working on yourselves so you can be prepared when that person comes. To prepare means to do the necessary work in order to succeed in the long run. I pray you have started to do the work and started to become content within this season. Trust me, it may feel like a lifetime, but it actually only lasts a moment if you believe it so. I pray this book has taught you that although you are in a season of singleness you can still live your life fulfilled and that you can still see and do the things you want to do. It may seem weird to go out to a restaurant or a movie by yourself, but what is crazy is to not do it because you lack the company. Doing those things for yourself is admirable because you know who you are and can stand firm in it. You do not need the validation from others. You gain that validation from God and that is all he ever wants us to do, is depend on him. So, do not look at your season as a "season of pause or idleness." The season you are in is a season of activity and forward movement. We are never alone on this path. We always have Jesus walking right alongside of us.

> *"For our light and momentary troubles are achieving for us an eternal glory that far outweighs them all. So we fix our eyes not on what is seen, but on what is unseen. For what is seen is temporary, but what is unseen is eternal." (2 Corinthians 4:17-18 NIV)*

God Bless you Sis, I'm praying for you.

www.ingramcontent.com/pod-product-compliance
Lightning Source LLC
Chambersburg PA
CBHW071421040426
42445CB00012BA/1240